LAZY LAMA LOOKS AT

Bodhichitta

Awakening compassion and wisdom

RINGU TULKU RINPOCHE

Number 4 in the Lazy Lama series

Bodhicharya
PUBLICATIONS
Awaken the heart by opening the mind

First Published in 2001 by
Bodhicharya Publications
24 Chester Street, Oxford, OX4 1SN, United Kingdom.
www.bodhicharya.org   email: publications@bodhicharya.org

Text © Ringu Tulku

Ringu Tulku asserts the moral right to be identified as the
author of this work. Please do not reproduce any part of this
book without permission from the publisher.

ISBN 978-0-9576398-5-0

Second Edition. 2014.

First transcribed and edited by Cait Collins 1998.

Typesetting & Design by Paul O'Connor at Judo Design, Ireland.

Printed on recycled paper by Imprint Digital, Devon, UK.

Cover Image: ©Getty Images
Internal illustrations: Robin Bath
Lazy Lama logo: Dr Conrad Harvey & Rebecca O'Connor

Editor's Preface

This is the fourth in the Lazy Lama series. It is based on two talks given by Ringu Tulku Rinpoche in Chichester in July 2000, at the request of Bodhicharya Buddhist Group.

I would like to thank from my heart Ringu Tulku Rinpoche for his warmth, generosity, and inexhaustible patience in communicating the Dharma with grace and humour and in a way that brings it to life and makes it seem like the most natural thing in the world – so, however much or little we can do, we can just 'do it now; why not?'

Cait Collins
2001

Bodhichitta

I think the starting point of the spiritual path is the understanding that we can transform ourselves. Our innate qualities, like loving-kindness, compassion, and wisdom, and our abilities to help ourselves and others can be cultivated. We can begin to engage in spiritual practice when we see that, besides whatever outer actions we may take to improve our life, there's also some inner work we can do: we can work on our mind to change the way we experience ourselves and our world. In Buddhist terms, each of us has the potential to become a buddha or an enlightened being by fully developing or fully awakening the natural qualities and abilities we already have within us.

Although many of the problems we encounter can be dealt with or put right, inevitably there will be some we can neither fix nor escape. The great spiritual masters of the past, including the Buddha, have faced the question that confronts us all: Is there anything we can do about these unavoidable sufferings?

If we can see that the major part of the difficulties and sufferings we experience is due to the way we look at and react to things and events, we can also see that if we could somehow transform or shift our habitual way of perceiving and relating to them, then our actual experience of them could change. The understandings and practices we find in the great spiritual traditions of the world offer us methods by which we can try to change our experience of events or circumstances by working on our way of perceiving and reacting to them.

Within a Buddhist context, spiritual practice or Dharma practice can begin when we not only glimpse the possibility of this transformation but are ready to look for ways to achieve it and actively try to work towards it. Our deciding to make this effort imparts a profound direction and purpose to our life. In the Buddhist tradition it can develop into what is called 'taking refuge' in the Buddha, Dharma, and Sangha, which is really the defining act of a Buddhist, not only marking the point at which we 'become a Buddhist' but also comprising the entire ongoing practice of Buddhism.

'Bodhichitta' [Sanskrit: *bodhicitta*] is a Sanskrit word that literally means 'mind of awakening'. We can think of bodhichitta as a natural extension of refuge: taking refuge means deciding to work towards fulfilling our own potential to transform our own experience and become free from fear and suffering, while developing bodhichitta expands our aim and practice to include all other beings. It is basically a kind of great compassion which is combined with understanding or wisdom. While compassion generally means wishing that a being or beings may be free of suffering, bodhichitta is that same wish combined with an understanding of the possibility of its actually being fulfilled. The compassion and wisdom aspects of bodhichitta, also termed relative and ultimate bodhichitta, need to be developed more or less simultaneously. They are like the two wings of a bird; if you cultivate one without the other you'll be like a bird with only one wing, going round in circles!

Relative Bodhichitta

Relative bodhichitta can be described in terms of a great compassion which is limitless in four ways, called the 'four immeasurables'. The first 'immeasurable' is the wish that all sufferings, without exception, may be utterly extinguished. Secondly, we are not just talking about all the sufferings of one person, or a few people, but all the sufferings of all sentient beings; not just human beings but every single sentient being of whatever kind throughout existence. Thirdly, it is not enough just to wish that all sentient beings without exception have no suffering at all, but also we wish that they may all attain unlimited perfect wellbeing or peace or freedom. Finally, we don't just wish that all beings may have immeasurable happiness or wellbeing temporarily, but for ever, immutably. So there is no limit to our aspirations, and no inequality or partiality. We're not saying, 'Well, OK, I'd like everyone to be free from their problems, but I want some – such as my family or friends – to do better than others!'

We combine this ideal compassion with an understanding of how it is possible for us to work towards transforming ourselves, and therefore, by extension, of how it is also possible for others to do likewise. The next step is to develop a strong sense of purpose or intention which includes a feeling of personal responsibility – 'I will work towards this aim' – motivated by the compassionate wish to be able to help others do the same.

In the Buddhist tradition, a person who has developed such a sense of purpose very deeply is called a bodhisattva [Sanskrit: *bodhisattva*]. 'Bodhi' means knowledge, wisdom, awakening, or enlightenment; while 'sattva' means one who has courage, has heart, or has aspiration. A bodhisattva is somebody who has the heart to work towards enlightenment, the ultimate freedom, for the sake of all beings. It is a great aspiration which includes tremendous courage and determination. There is a kind of heroic dimension to it; such a person is a hero, in a way!

Whatever we want to do in life, the first step is to have an aspiration. If we have an aspiration we will naturally start to work towards fulfilling it, whether more or less consciously or unconsciously. This is why it is considered so important to admire the bodhisattva ideal and to start cultivating the beginnings of a bodhichitta aspiration ourselves; even just a thought of it would be a very strong practice, while to succeed in actually generating a genuine bodhichitta aspiration would be a tremendous, wonderful achievement.

Of course, we must accept that we are not really bodhisattvas right now. Even if I have taken formal bodhisattva vows it doesn't mean I have become a bodhisattva; it means I have made a commitment saying that I would like to become a bodhisattva and would like to start to work on the bodhisattva path. I haven't suddenly become some kind of a saint, completely free of selfishness and anger – that doesn't happen so easily!

So we start by trying to work in this direction little by little, first generating some loving-kindness as expressed in a traditional prayer-wish such as:

May all sentient beings have happiness and the causes of happiness;
May all sentient beings be free from sufferings and the causes of sufferings.

This allows our attitude towards ourselves and others to become a little softer, more open. Ideally we try to have a spirit of kindness and helpfulness towards everyone – or at least, even if we are unable or don't want to help, we don't bear them any ill will. We wish that they may meet no suffering and may attain all the good things they desire.

Helping others with bodhichitta motivation doesn't only mean helping in obviously 'spiritual' ways, or overlooking the little everyday things to focus only on the grand ultimate goal of total liberation or enlightenment. It means helping in many ways, for great and small and long-term and short-term benefits. Just as I want everything to go well for me, whether in large or small matters, lasting or temporary, so does everybody else want that for themselves, and we try to help in every way we can.

What we actually do to help is not necessarily the most important aspect in the bodhisattva path. The intention or attitude underlying what we do is regarded as more important because that becomes the basis, the motivation for all our actions. If you have the bodhichitta motivation then whatever you do will be of help, because your whole purpose is to use whatever resources you have in a way that is beneficial to you and to others. We can use only whatever circumstances and methods are available to us at any moment, but as long as we have the clear intention of helping others and ourselves we can make good use of whatever understanding we have and whatever means we can muster at the time. Anything we do that is good for ourselves and for others is a positive act, and if we do it with the wish that we may become able to do more, to gain more understanding and wisdom, and to become more effective, then we are moving towards a bodhisattva attitude.

Sometimes people mistakenly think that compassion may be all right for others but is not so good for oneself. If I'm too compassionate and helpful people will take advantage of me because they see me as a pushover! But compassion means wanting the best for everyone – myself as well as others – and I don't have to try to do everything everyone asks. I do as much as I can, but if I can't help, then I can't help. But even if I can't actually help now, I can maintain the wish to be able to help in the future. This is the bodhisattva's skilful means of training; it isn't necessarily skilful to just give everything away.

There is a rather horrible story which illustrates this point. A man who generated the wish to become a great bodhisattva made a vow to give people whatever they wanted; he would never refuse anybody anything they asked for. So of course everybody came and asked for this and that, and as he was a rich man he could give them whatever they wanted. This went on for quite some time, until one day a particularly difficult customer came along and asked if it was really true that he would give whatever was asked of him.

'That's right. I'm a bodhisattva. I'm happy to give everyone whatever they want.'

'Then give me your right hand.'

The 'bodhisattva' didn't hesitate: he asked for a knife and he cut off his right hand and gave it. But the man refused to accept it – in fact he was furious! In India the left hand is regarded as unclean. They're very particular about it: you can't even pass the salt or pepper with your left hand – people won't take it.

'You can't give me something with your left hand! That's disgusting!' he shouted.

And according to the story the would-be bodhisattva was so shocked and discouraged by this incident that he abandoned his efforts altogether: 'People are impossible to please,' he said. 'That's the end of my bodhichitta!'

So it was a useless thing to do, just giving unintelligently without discriminating between what was and wasn't beneficial, and practising compassion shouldn't be like that.

I think it is also important to understand

that practising compassion doesn't mean just trying to please people. It is trying to be helpful, to benefit others, to improve matters. If somebody asked you to do something destructive – 'Please break my leg' – you wouldn't say, 'Sure, why not? I never say no!' would you? So it's like that: it's not just being nice and doing whatever people ask, but intelligently wanting to help. Maybe someone – perhaps a child – might benefit from being chided. It isn't being unkind to them; it's actually being kinder than just giving in to whatever they demand. Of course it may mean they won't like you very much at that moment, but it is no good wanting to be liked by everybody; that isn't the idea!

Another point we need to be clear about is that our practice of compassion is not dependent on whether or not we like the other person. Sometimes people think that it is impossible to be compassionate towards all beings because we can't like all beings. Of course we can't like everybody! How can I like people who have been harming others? I can't like them, or admire them; but still I don't need to wish them harm. Rather, I can wish that they would change and would stop harming themselves and others; I can wish that they could find peace and freedom from their painful and destructive states of mind. It is possible to do that for everyone, even those who have done terrible things to others.

We could say that kindness to others is based on our kindness towards ourselves. If we don't know how to wish ourselves well, how can we wish others well? I think it is a mistake to criticise ourselves for wanting our own wellbeing. If we wish ourselves and others well, what can go wrong? Everyone benefits. Whatever I do, I try to see whether it will be good for myself now and later, and good for others now and later. If, as far as I can see, it seems to be all right, then I'll do it. If I see that it may seem advantageous for me but would be harmful to others, then I look for another, less damaging way of doing it. And if I see that it may be good for others but would be very harmful to me, then also I try to avoid it. Perhaps sometimes there could be a great benefit to others at some cost to myself; then it is up to me to judge whether I'm ready to sacrifice some of my own interests for the sake of others. If I can make that sacrifice without too much regret, then, all right, I can do it; but if I find that I would regret it too much, then I would do better to acknowledge that I'm not yet ready for it.

The more we become accustomed to doing something, the more our ability to do it improves. This applies both physically and mentally, doesn't it? We can train ourselves through practice to become stronger. The more we practise compassion and goodwill, the easier it becomes; it is the same with becoming accustomed to any feelings or states of mind, whether worry and anger or joy and peacefulness. For example, we try to feel peaceful and relaxed when we practise meditation, and that is part of the training. Training in the spiritual path means practising, exercising, again and again. It's like cultivating a habit: if you do something often enough, it becomes your habit; and, eventually, as your habit becomes stronger, it becomes second nature. According to Buddhist teachings, and this is borne out by the experience of many great masters, we are in fact basically all right at the deepest level, in our true nature; our distorted way of perceiving and relating to the world and all our problems have come about due to our conditioning. This conditioning is habitual, in a way, and we can take a first step towards overcoming it by cultivating a different habit – the habit of being kind, relaxed, peaceful and joyful. And the more we do it, the more accustomed to it we'll become and the easier it will be, until our compassion and wisdom become so strong that we will be ready for anything!

So we start by working at our own level, not expecting too much of ourselves to begin with but acknowledging our shortcomings, especially our selfishness, and wanting to develop our positive qualities because we can see that to do so will be good for us and for others.

We can use reflection and reasoning to help us progress in this way. We can understand that to wish others harm does no-one any good; and why do something which does no-one any good? Take for instance anger, in the sense of the opposite of loving-kindness. We know that anger is not a comfortable experience: nobody would say, 'Oh, I was very happy this morning – I was so angry.' But still we get angry if someone annoys us: 'I'm angry because this person has done something.' The basic concept is that this person wants to harm me; therefore I am angry. Whether or not he or she actually could harm me is a different matter, and of course I should do whatever is necessary to prevent his harming me. But, in any case, if I continue being resentful and angry then in a way I'm working for my enemy because I'm helping him to make me uncomfortable. He wanted to make me unhappy and my being angry is helping him to achieve that! If I didn't become angry then I would feel happier and therefore could actually thwart his attempt to harm me.

Another line of reasoning might be to understand how the person who is behaving destructively is influenced by circumstances: in a way he or she is like someone who is sick, or maybe drunk, acting out of confusion and not in control of his behaviour. If we understand that someone is acting out of confusion or sickness, then we don't get angry with him; we feel compassion instead.

The point here is that if we can begin to understand a situation we can change our way of perceiving it and reacting to it. If we just look at it from our usual limited point of view, from our own side only, we'll react according to our usual habit; but if we look from the other side, or take a broader view, then we can open up other possible ways of responding. Through understanding how and why people behave as they do, and how much suffering and selfishness there is in all of us and how much further suffering that brings, we can develop more compassion for others and more patience with their destructive actions.

This understanding will also help us to appreciate the kindness and other good qualities we find in others. Sometimes we have problems with others because our expectations are too high: if we expect others to be always nice, kind, compassionate, generous, and wise, then of course we'll have problems, because people can't be like that! Maybe someone is much more compassionate and generous and kind than I am, but even so she can't be completely saintly all the time! And then if I see a small fault, maybe an angry word or a little unkindness, I'm very disappointed and unhappy and I can't tolerate it. But if I understand that others are more or less like me, having some kindness and compassion but also lots of selfishness, faults, and weaknesses, then I will appreciate any little kindness I receive: despite her having the weaknesses we both have, still she has been able to be kind to me. It's a great thing, a matter for rejoicing!

Rejoicing is much emphasised in Buddhism; it is another aspect of compassion. Our habitual tendency is such that while it is not so hard to empathise regarding someone's suffering, it is more difficult to do so regarding their success. We tend to feel jealousy: 'She's doing so well; I should be doing just as well or even better.' We are not very happy about somebody doing better than we are! Developing the quality of rejoicing means cultivating the habit of being happy when someone else is happy, delighting in another's success. If we can do this then we can be happy without ourselves succeeding in anything!

Instead of suffering with jealousy we can be happy. We can be happy all the time, because at every moment somebody somewhere must be doing something or achieving something we can rejoice in!

Rejoicing is considered a very positive deed. The Buddhist definition of a positive deed is one which results in happiness and wellbeing for yourself and others. By rejoicing in others' success you feel better, while if you are jealous and resentful not only does that not make you any more successful, but on top of that you are unhappy – for no purpose. What is the use of feeling miserable for nothing?

Rejoicing is also considered to be a kind of compassion because you are not only feeling goodwill towards those who are suffering or are worse off than yourself, but also towards those who are more fortunate than you. If you just send your goodwill to people less fortunate than yourself, it is as though you are discriminating against some beings; then you don't have universal goodwill or consistent compassion. Rejoicing enables you to feel the same goodwill towards everyone, whether more or less fortunate than yourself.

This steadiness leads to what is termed equanimity: you have goodwill towards everyone, whether better off, worse off, or equal to you; whether your friends or not your friends. You have no ill will. Your mind is, we can say, luminous; there is no dark spot in it.

So in this way we can cultivate the wish to do what's best for ourselves and others, and as we become more accustomed to it so it will grow stronger and stronger until eventually we experience it as our natural way of being; and in that way we can gradually become more like real bodhisattvas.

In the Buddhist tradition there are vows we can take when we feel ready to make a commitment to the bodhisattva path. We state our intention in a prayer which we then repeat frequently to remind ourselves of our motivation: that we want to help to liberate all sentient beings and that we are dedicating all our activities towards that purpose. As we saw earlier, the bodhisattva commitment is a natural extension of our Buddhist refuge, our personal direction or purpose in life. I think it is very important to have a great, profound purpose: if we have a strong sense of purpose we will never feel completely lost, whatever we do or in whatever circumstances we find ourselves. What could be greater than the bodhisattva motivation, the expression of limitless love and compassion? If we can make that our long-term purpose then everything we do will be directed towards it and our entire life will be meaningful.

Without any clear purpose in our life, we won't know where we are going or what we are doing; we'll be lost, just wandering round and round. Finding a clear and constructive direction is a very important step towards finding our own inner peace and loving-kindness; and from that beginning maybe the transformation of the world can happen. It's not impossible! If at first a few people, then more people, then everybody wants to help each other, then tomorrow the world could be a better place. It's not just a dream, wishing that others would change; it is starting with what I myself can actually do right now, at my own level, to work on myself. I can't force anyone else, but I can do something myself; and if I do it then maybe others will be encouraged to do it too.

There is a story about this. I heard it in Edinburgh, but I don't know where it comes from originally. A priest requested a particular epitaph to be carved on his tombstone. He wanted it to read like this: 'I was a very enthusiastic priest, and I wanted to change the world. I prayed to God, "May I have the power and the wisdom to change the world." I prayed and prayed, but after a long time I realised that nothing had changed. Then I understood that first I must change my near and dear ones: if I could change them, then they would be an example for the world, and the world would change. So I prayed to God, "Please give me the power and the wisdom to change my near and dear ones, so that the world may change." I prayed like this, and I tried hard all my life, but when I was very old I realised that no-one had changed. At last I understood that first I must change myself, and then, perhaps, following my example, my near and dear ones might change, and then, perhaps, following their example, the world might change. But now it is too late.'

So we start with ourselves, and, however much or little we can do, we try to do it now; because how else to begin?

Ultimate Bodhichitta

Up until now we have been discussing relative bodhichitta – the compassion wing of the bird, you could say. Now we'll go on to look at ultimate bodhichitta, the wisdom wing. We need to develop them both if we want to fly!

Real wisdom or ultimate wisdom is not just knowledge in the sense of collecting information. It is much deeper than that. It is an experience of the way things really are, an experience of ultimate truth, you can call it. It is understanding – not just in an intellectual way, but deeply, experientially realising – the way things are, the way you are, or what you are. It means realising or awakening to your true nature and experiencing this completely.

Wisdom and compassion are closely linked, and as long as we are lacking wisdom our compassion will be incomplete. Sometimes our wish to help is not really motivated by compassion for the other person but by our own need to feel good or to feel important. In a way that's all right; without wisdom this kind of weakness is inevitable. It's natural; we are all selfish. If I say I am not selfish, I am either lying or deceiving myself! Without wisdom I can't be anything but selfish.

I think it is important to understand and acknowledge that we, as worldly beings, or, in Buddhist terminology, 'samsaric beings', have weaknesses and are selfish. We have some compassion and kindness, but also we are selfish. When I can fully accept my own selfishness and understand that there is likewise selfishness in everybody, then I am actually being honest and realistic, and then I won't be so shocked when somebody behaves in a way that is a little selfish and unkind. Often we have unrealistic expectations, expecting people to be always nice and kind. For example, sometimes people visit Buddhist centres expecting everybody there to be peaceful, kind, and compassionate; because that's what Buddhism teaches, isn't it? But the people in the centres are not always like that! Of course not! People come to Buddhist centres because they want to become peaceful, kind, and compassionate; if they were already like that, there would be no need for them to come to the centres! As long as we are in this unenlightened state we'll have these problems; that is why we want to change and that is what we need to work on. We need to understand and to accept this, otherwise we'll expect too much from ourselves and from others.

I believe that the necessity to overcome our self-centredness is the central message of all the major world religions. What are the characteristics of people generally considered to be 'holy'? Highly learned people are not necessarily holy; nor are those who are powerful or materially successful. I think that those who are thought of as 'holy' all have in common the characteristics of unselfishness and generosity; they have been able to transcend their self-centredness and therefore are able to give to others.

The ability to transcend our self-centredness can come from the wisdom of knowing ourselves, knowing who and what it is we call 'me'. This is the most important practice, the essential search, because as long as we are confused about who or what we are, the nature of our existence, or the nature of reality, you could call it, we will continue to have problems and suffering. As long as we have the exaggerated and distorted sense of self we have at present, we will inevitably be self-centred and selfish. Our way of reacting and behaving will be from the point of view of 'me' at the centre of 'my' world: 'me' and 'other'. In a way we're confronting everybody and everything: it's either good for me or not good for me; my friend or my enemy. Then we react accordingly: I want it or I don't want it; I run after it or away from it; I try to hold onto it or push it away. When we are repeatedly reacting like that then our experience consists of little else but fear and clinging. That cycle of repetitive reaction based on attachment and aversion is called samsara [Sanskrit: *samsara*], and the only way out of it is through wisdom.

It is difficult to express or explain what is meant by the wisdom of understanding the nature of reality because it must be directly experienced by each person for himself or herself. And that is not such an easy thing to do. To experience it fully would be to become enlightened.

It is really the only way we can get to the root of our fear and insecurity. If we can deeply understand the nature of reality we will realise that there is no need of fear, because we will find there is nothing in us which can be destroyed. We will see how the body is comprised of parts, such as the five elements, which are always changing and which will naturally dissolve. If I search throughout my body I can't find anything I can point to and say 'this is me'. And what is my mind? The mind is my experience of the here and now; it can't be grasped – it would be like trying to catch the wind, or hold onto flowing water. The mind is a beginningless and endless continuum, changing moment to moment; you could say it is already dying each moment. So what is there to be destroyed?

To experience this clearly is to understand that there is nothing to fear. It is a little like realising that there is no need to feel insecure because there is no such thing as security! If you understand that there can be no security because there is nothing to be secured, then you can no longer feel insecure. When you gain that understanding deeply, then there is no more fear. The concept of 'insecurity' can only be maintained if there is a concept of 'security'.

This realisation is a liberation: as we realise there is no need to react with fear and attachment it's as though we've been freed or awakened from a bad dream. Not only that: because there is no longer any need to strive for my own gain, genuine compassion can arise. If I have nothing to fear and therefore nothing to gain for myself then I am free to work solely for others; if I don't have to worry about my own problems then I am free to help others overcome their problems. This is the real compassion that comes out of wisdom, the wisdom and compassion in union; this is the ideal we are working towards, the ultimate bodhichitta.

Now, how to go about achieving that, step-by-step? As we have already discussed, the relative bodhichitta, the compassion, is something we can begin to understand and gradually develop through practice; and this ultimate bodhichitta can also be developed by increasing our understanding and by practising. Developing our understanding is a stepping-stone to generating true compassion and wisdom.

Since wisdom is the experience of knowing yourself and discovering your true nature, it requires a kind of introspection. It is an insight, a seeing-in, and the path prescribed in Buddhism to achieve this is meditation, specifically insight meditation.

There are 100,000 different kinds of Buddhist meditation techniques, but they can be broadly categorised into two types: calm-abiding and insight meditation.

The calm-abiding meditation is called in Tibetan shi-nay [*zhi gnas*], in Sanskrit shamata [*samatha*]. Its function is to calm the mind so it becomes more relaxed and more stable. In a way it is learning to relax, learning to be yourself, to be natural; not so stressed and conditioned. You could say it's learning just to be. Learning how to relax and how to calm the mind is the basis of meditation. Usually we're busy, caught up in the activities of the five senses; we're always seeing something, hearing something. We are almost over-powered by the five senses, so there is no time or space for us to begin to look at ourselves, or allow ourselves just to be natural. It is like a continual bombardment, like watching those television cartoons that are so fast the images come flying at us, zip-zip-zip. It is difficult to be aware of ourselves because we are so bombarded with our sensory perceptions, but if we can slow the process down a bit we can begin to become aware of our true nature more clearly. That is why it is said that the calmer the mind, the clearer it becomes; and as the mind becomes clearer we can become aware of our true nature. The true nature of our mind is clarity, but we just can't see it because we are too busy.

When we practise this shinay meditation we may gently focus our attention on the breathing, or we may just rest lightly in the present moment; either way, we don't allow ourselves to be overwhelmed or carried away by thoughts and emotions or sensory perceptions. There is a saying: 'Bring your body to your seat, bring your mind to your body, and bring peace to your mind.' So we try to relax like that.

When you have found a little bit of calmness you can practise the insight meditation: looking at the nature of the mind which is calm, so therefore clear. Then your mind can become clearer and clearer and you can see exactly what or how you are, in an experiential way. It is not easy to do! But if you can see that completely clearly then you see the nature of your mind, and that experience is what we call wisdom. Wisdom means completely seeing ourselves clearly without any mistake or distortion.

Complete wisdom is necessarily accompanied by compassion, and the union of total compassion and wisdom is called enlightenment. A buddha is someone who has developed his or her compassion and wisdom to the utmost. We call it enlightenment or awakening or realisation because it is not the case that we acquire something we didn't have before, but rather that we realise or wake up to something we just hadn't realised. We are not acquiring anything, we are just seeing the way we actually are, or the way everything really is. It has actually always been like that but we haven't noticed it!

I think I will stop here, and if you have any questions we can discuss them.

Discussion

Questioner: Sometimes we can see changes occurring in ourselves, but it isn't easy to maintain them. Is that where we need compassion towards ourselves?

Rinpoche: I think so. Of course, we are changing all the time anyway; everything is changing all the time. But our long-established habits are not easy to change. It's no use being too impatient; we've been like this all our life, maybe even for many lives, so we can't expect to change so easily. If even a habit we have acquired quite recently in this life, like smoking, can be very difficult to give up, we can't expect it to be easy to give up the habitual tendencies of many lifetimes! But we make an effort, little by little, without expecting that we will become completely transformed in a few days or months or even a few years, and if there is a little improvement then I think we can be happy about it; we can encourage ourselves and maybe even congratulate ourselves a bit! Also, it isn't always easy to judge our own progress. Long-term change can be very slow. We may have done a little meditation and had some experiences and think we've really changed, but these kind of changes are only temporary, because then we change again!

Questioner: I find the idea of helping people quite confusing. It seems almost arrogant to think we can know what's best for someone else. I wonder if helping someone is necessarily the best thing for that person in a particular situation; maybe he or she could learn from whatever is happening. Can you shed any more light on the idea of helping people?

Rinpoche: Of course, you can't help people without bringing in your own ideas and understandings. For example, you think that someone needs food, so you bring food, or you think he or she needs clothes so you bring clothes. I don't think there's anything wrong with your doing what you think is best for others like that. Maybe it would be wrong if they didn't want your help but you tried to force it on them; but even then it could be that they don't know what they need – that can also be the case. Someone might be sick and need medicine but not want to take it; then if you know that it would be helpful maybe you could still try to give it.

How effective you can be is largely dependent on the other person: it is difficult to help someone who doesn't help himself or herself. Some people are easily helped: you just give a little assistance and they can really benefit in many ways; but some people, whatever you do, it's no use.

The most important thing for your own development is that you try to help as much as you can. Buddhists like to talk about the 'middle path', and I think there is a middle path to follow here. Try to do it in a balanced way, neither too much nor too little; then you can continue for a longer period. If you try to do too much you can get burnt out, and then you have no energy left to do anything.

Questioner: What if the person you're trying to help doesn't know she has a problem?

Rinpoche: It's difficult to say. If this person doesn't think she has a problem but you think she has, maybe you are wrong. Perhaps she doesn't have a problem; perhaps you have a problem because you think she has a problem! It could be like that! Or maybe she has a problem but doesn't recognise it or won't acknowledge it; then if you know how to help, you may be able to help. I don't think we can generalise about it. But I think it is important to accept that you can't help everyone; not everyone will want your help or be receptive to what you have to offer. There is no need for you to try to impose your help on someone who doesn't want it; you can give it to those who want to be helped.

Questioner: I'm new to Buddhism, and I have several questions.

Firstly, was this concept of bodhichitta that you've been describing taught by the Buddha himself? Is there a scripture in Sanskrit? Or was it developed over time by Buddhist priests?

The reason I'm asking is because I'm wondering about differences in the cultural environment and upbringing of Eastern people compared with ourselves in the West. For instance, when you talk about perceiving and being compassionate towards others' needs, for those in the East – forgive me for the generalisation – the needs might be more material and physical, whereas in the West people talk about spiritual crisis. And I'm wondering whether this concept of bodhichitta would apply in the context of the actual physical suffering of people who are so materially impoverished.

Also I'd like to ask, do you think there is a fundamental difference between Eastern and Western people regarding the ease with which they can respond to Buddhist teaching? Does the burden of Western culture on people like ourselves make it more difficult for us to be receptive to it?

Rinpoche: There is a written scripture of the Buddha's teachings. Of course his original spoken teachings were in an Indian language. They were written down later in two languages: first in Pali and then in Sanskrit. The Sanskrit version was translated into Tibetan from the 8th century of the Christian era onwards for about 200 or 300 years; it has been collected into about 100 volumes in Tibetan. The teachings were not written down while the Buddha was alive, but later; it is said that after the Buddha died, the monks who had heard his teachings recited what they had heard and then they started writing them down. They were written down gradually, maybe all completed by around the 1st century or 2nd century. And of course there were many commentaries written by others on the Buddha's teachings, and a lot of literature has been produced over the years, and different philosophical schools and Buddhist traditions have come about. Regarding the basics, such as this topic we've been talking about, there isn't much difference among the different Buddhist traditions. The bodhichitta teachings are emphasised in the mahayana tradition, or Northern Buddhism as it is sometimes called, that is found in China, Japan, Tibet, Mongolia, and Korea; but you also find them in the other traditions.

Regarding your other question, I think it is true that in certain parts of the Eastern world there is a great need of material help, while in the West now there is more need of what can be called, perhaps, spiritual or mental help. But when we talk about helping beings, we are not making such a distinction; the teachings talk about both material and spiritual help.

I think that people all over the world are basically the same. We all share a similar experience; we feel the same sorrow, the same joy, and if we have a problem we feel unhappy. The differences are at the cultural and linguistic level, which is I think a superficial layer. I am not saying it isn't important; it is actually very important, because that is the level of communication. We all have a certain way of thinking and behaving which comes from our own culture and our own background, and of course language is full of pitfalls – you discover that especially forcefully when you try to communicate in a language which is not your first language! But still I think this layer is quite a shallow one, and if we go a little deeper we'll find the similarities are much greater than the differences.

Questioner: Something I find very difficult is how when we open up a little bit to this feeling of compassion, we also open up to the many terrible things happening in the world, which otherwise we might perhaps be able to ignore or turn away from. I find it very shocking and distressing. I can't bear to watch the news on television any more; it's just too much to take. When you talked about the meaning of the word 'bodhisattva' you said it included the connotation of courageousness or having courage. Please would you say something about that courage?

Rinpoche: I think that when we begin to gain a deeper understanding of the suffering of beings we start to become more aware of it, and that is why we want to do something to help. If we really acknowledge and accept the extent and gravity of it, then when we see some particular instance of suffering we are not too shocked.

If you expect things to be not too bad, then when you are confronted by some suffering it really shocks you. But if you understand that there is so much suffering all around, and have that understanding deeply grounded in you, then when you see some specific instance of it, whether on the television or whatever, it won't bowl you over. I am not saying that you should become indifferent to it, but I think the basic acceptance and understanding of the extent of the problem is very important, because it isn't helpful to let yourself become too shocked by suffering. Your understanding of the depth of the suffering that goes on should become the basis of your wanting to help, and your being confronted by suffering shouldn't discourage you but should strengthen your determination to help. Suffering is happening all the time, whether you like it or not. Maybe you need to become a bit more used to it, like doctors and nurses have to become accustomed to dealing with sick and injured people; at first it might be difficult, but then after you've done it a few times you become used to it and can work more effectively to help your patients. So basically I think the problem is that your perception of the world is a bit too good!

Questioner: Part of the problem is that we are so flooded with horrific things through the media. 'Chicken crosses the road and reaches the other side' isn't news; it's 'chicken crosses the road and is killed'. And this is all the news we get – it's completely unbalanced – and it becomes increasingly difficult to take it; you just want to get away from it all.

Rinpoche: I agree! I once went to an exhibition of prize-winning newspaper photos in Amsterdam. It was terrible – full of chopped heads and other horrible images. I was offered a souvenir booklet of the photos and I said, 'Please, no! I don't want it, thank you very much!'

But I think there may be something good about all this horror in the media: it means that when terrible things happen, it's news. That's good, isn't it? The fact that it is news means it isn't an everyday occurrence; it's unusual and it's shocking. If good news becomes the news, then is the time to worry, because then things would be really bad.

Questioner: Isn't there some confusion here between compassion and sensitivity? If we're shocked by what we see in the newspaper, isn't that sensitivity rather than compassion? We should be reacting more with compassion than with sensitivity, shouldn't we?

Rinpoche: I think you can be sensitive towards anything, while compassion is specifically wanting to help. You can be very sensitive and be compassionate, or you can be less sensitive but still be compassionate. I think it is also possible to be sensitive and not very compassionate. Of course it is not good to be too insensitive or you wouldn't care whatever happens. But I think it is better not to be over-sensitive or you make things very painful for yourself, and it doesn't help anybody.

Questioner: What actually is the 'self'? Please would you talk more about the true nature or ultimate nature of the self.

Rinpoche: : It's a very difficult question! What is the self? It is much discussed in Buddhist philosophy, but it is really something you can only find out for yourself. Sometimes it is said there is no 'self'. Some philosophers, for example Nagarjuna, talk about shunyata [Sanskrit: *sunyata*], the emptiness of the self. They say that if you look closely at anything you'll find that what you thought was just one fixed thing ctually interrelated, interdependent, and changing; you can't find one thing which is independently, individually there, not dependent on anything else. Therefore it is said there is no 'self' as such which exists independently. This is how the Buddhist philosophy of interdependence or dependent arising comes about, which you could say is one of the main Buddhist philosophies.

I don't really know how best to discuss it. If I talk from the philosophical point of view it becomes too conceptual or theoretical, and I don't want to do that because then you might think, 'Oh, that's what Buddhists believe.' And that's not really the point; it isn't useful. Of course when you describe something, you have to describe it according to your own experience, and then that can become a philosophy. But actually it could be described in many different ways. It isn't very helpful to say 'It's like this,' because it isn't really 'like this.' It is something which must be experienced.

The Buddha used five words to express his experience of realisation: deep; peaceful; simple, or not falling to extremes; luminous; and uncreated or uncompounded. In Tibetan it is zab, shi, tö-del, ö-sel, du-ma-che [zab, zhi, spros bral, 'od gsal, 'dus ma byas]. There are thousands of volumes of explanations and arguments about the nature of the self or the nature of reality, but basically it has to be experienced. You have to look at yourself. You have to develop stability and calmness and then, within that calmness, you have to look; and then that's it.

You can get an idea of it through studying and trying to understand explanations and descriptions – 'Maybe it's like this' – but that is still just a concept. Some Buddhist philosophical systems use questioning as a method to demolish or deconstruct the concepts you cling to: 'Is it like this? It can't be like this. Then is it like this? No, it can't be like this.' You use this method to clear away all the possibilities until you are brought to an understanding that's beyond your grasping and conceptualising. That's the madhyamika [Sanskrit: *madhyamika*], the middle way philosophy. But in the end it is actually something to be experienced through meditation, through direct, non-conceptual experience that can't be learnt from others.

Questioner: When you start meditating, sometimes one of the first things you get in touch with is not peace but agitation. It can be quite difficult to be able to hold on for long enough to get beyond it in order to be able to do what you're talking about in terms of being able to look at the nature of self. Can you say something about how to deal with agitation in meditation?

Rinpoche: It is said that the first sign of progress in meditation is what is called the waterfall experience. A waterfall is very forceful. When you begin to meditate you notice many things going on in your mind and you begin to see how distracted you are, or how agitated, maybe you can call it. That is called the rushing waterfall experience, and it is said to be the first stage of progress. Usually we are not aware of how busy our mind is and how much restlessness we have, so this experience is actually a sign that we are beginning to calm down! And this is the time, they say, that most meditators have difficulties and some people give up trying to meditate at this point because it's too much. So you can see this stage as progress; when you try to meditate and you feel that you can't meditate at all, it's a good sign! If you can get through this stage your practice can go more smoothly. But of course progress is never completely smooth; it is always up and down.

Questioner: I feel very reassured by your saying that. Sometimes it has felt like being in a washing machine! I have a question about how much meditation to aim for each day in order for it to have a real value. I try to do at least a little every day, but what's your view about a suitable amount of time to aim at?

Rinpoche: I don't think there is any time limit, either minimum or maximum. The more you can do, the better; but you need to take into account your day-to-day situation, your health, and your mental disposition. And it isn't only the amount of time you spend on meditation that matters, but also the understanding of how to do it. You can't learn that from someone else; you can only learn it by doing it. You need to find the right balance. If you concentrate too much then you actually become more tense and more agitated; and you don't need more tension – you have that all the time anyway! But neither should it be so loose that the usual tendencies take over and you're distracted and don't know what's going on. So finding the balance is very important, and this you must find for yourself by practising.

Learning how to meditate can take a long time; although of course you can't generalise – it varies from person to person. Practising meditation isn't like doing anything else. Usually, whatever we do, the more effort we put into it the better the result, but it doesn't work like that with meditation. For meditation it's a case of the less effort, the better. It's difficult for us to practise without effort because we're not used to it. Trying to do something without doing anything – how to do that?! But if you can learn how to do that, it becomes easier; you've found the secret! Then you can meditate for as long as you like; otherwise, if you don't know how to do it, trying to do too much meditation will itself bring stress.

This is why it is recommended to go slowly at first, according to how you feel, and with many breaks. Whatever period you do – one hour, half an hour, 20 minutes – you take breaks within that period. I don't know why, or who made this 20 minute rule, but 20 minutes seems to have become a standard period all over the world! But whatever length of time you do, after a little bit you have a break. 'Break' here means just relaxing and taking a little rest, not getting up and making a cup of tea! It is even said that the meditation you do during the break can be better than the actual meditation; if we are trying too hard to meditate, then when we take a break we really rest and relax and that can be of more meditative value than the actual meditation.

Questioner: You're saying quality is as important as quantity?

Rinpoche: Yes, that's right.

Questioner: Is realisation a momentary event, or is it a continuum?

Rinpoche: Due to certain circumstances, such as being in a very natural state for a time, you can have a glimpse; but this experience doesn't last because your habitual mind comes back. This kind of experience is momentary, you can call it. But we don't call it realisation; it's just an experience.

Progress can be described in three stages.

The first can be called understanding; it's not a real experience, but a little bit of clarity. It can still be conceptual: 'It must be like this, there's no other way it could be; that's it.' It can also come about from learning and study.

The next step is the experience that comes about due to certain circumstances, such as a good, strong meditation. It may be a very powerful experience but it doesn't last; it is not a complete realisation. But then when that experience grows stronger and you are seeing it completely clearly, then that is the realisation, and that is not momentary. If you see it completely, it's just like that; it's nothing to do with momentary or continuous. You just know it. You know what you are; there is no defilement, nothing to cloud you. But even then it may take some time to become completely clear and stable.

Questioner: You were talking earlier about rejoicing in somebody else's good fortune. That must come from being content in yourself; otherwise you'd feel envious of somebody else who is achieving where you feel you've been under-achieving. Do you think it's possible to rejoice fully in other people's achievements without being completely self-content?

Rinpoche: Of course, if you are totally content, there is no reason not to rejoice in somebody else's success; and if you are not so content, it is natural to feel jealous and envious towards others. But this is where the training comes in. You reflect and reason: 'What benefit do I receive from this envy?' Feeling envious of someone else's success doesn't help you to get what you want; it just makes you unhappy. Who wants to feel unhappy? By rejoicing you feel good. So why not feel good instead of unhappy in the same circumstances? That is a learning; it's a habit. The habit now is to think, 'Oh, she has done well. That's not good; I should have done better.' But if you feel good it doesn't make your chances worse. You can still try to achieve whatever it is, can't you? There's nothing stopping you. If you rejoice you will feel good, and your rival will still be your friend; at least from your point of view. That is important: if you think of everybody as your friend, you'll feel happy. You can't control how others feel but you're in charge of how you feel. So rejoicing is good for you and for the other person.

Sometimes people think that if you lack envy and jealousy you'll lose your competitive edge and your will to succeed. I don't think that's right. You don't need to compete with another person, you can compete for excellence. If you're competing with others, then at best you'll just get a little ahead of your rivals, which means harming others and yourself for a very small aim; but if you're aiming for excellence then you don't need to hold back your friends or step on your friends on the way up the ladder. You can not only do better than your friends, you can be the best in the world! As the saying goes, 'There's always room at the top.' Whatever you're very good at, there is always space at the top; there is less space at the bottom!

I think it is better to work together with other people; if we can help each other it benefits everyone, while if we try to hold each other back it's not good for anyone. Acting with kindness doesn't kill your instinct of competitiveness, your will to improve. If people help each other, everybody can do better. Stones supporting each other can make a house; people helping each other can achieve great things.

Thank you all very much.

All my babbling,
In the name of Dharma
Has been set down faithfully
By my dear students of pure vision.

I pray that at least a fraction of the wisdom
Of those enlightened teachers
Who tirelessly trained me
Shines through this mass of incoherence.

May the sincere efforts of all those
Who have worked tirelessly
Result in spreading the true meaning of Dharma
To all who are inspired to know.

May this help dispel the darkness of ignorance
In the minds of all living beings
And lead them to complete realisation
Free from all fear.

Ringu Tulku

Acknowledgements

We would like to thank the students of Bodhicharya Buddhist Group for requesting and organising the events in Chichester and for contributing to them with enthusiasm and sincerity.

We also wish to thank the original team that produced the first edition of this book: Jude Tarrant, for design and layout; Robin Bath, for his drawings; Alison de Ledesma, for distribution; and Cait Collins, for transcribing and editing this book.

For this second edition we would like to thank: Paul O'Connor, for this new layout and design; Dr Conrad Harvey & Rebecca O'Connor, for the new Lazy Lama logo illustration; Rachel Moffitt, for distribution and proof reading.

About the Author

Ringu Tulku Rinpoche is a Tibetan Buddhist Master of the Kagyu Order. He was trained in all schools of Tibetan Buddhism under many great masters including HH the 16th Gyalwang Karmapa and HH Dilgo Khyentse Rinpoche. He took his formal education at Namgyal Institute of Tibetology, Sikkim and Sampurnananda Sanskrit University, Varanasi, India. He served as Tibetan Textbook Writer and Professor of Tibetan Studies in Sikkim for 25 years.

Since 1990, he has been travelling and teaching Buddhism and meditation in Europe, America, Canada, Australia and Asia. He participates in various interfaith and 'Science and Buddhism' dialogues and is the author of several books on Buddhist topics. These include Path to Buddhahood, Daring Steps, The Ri-me Philosophy of Jamgon Kongtrul the

Great, Confusion Arises as Wisdom, the Lazy Lama series and the Heart Wisdom series, as well as several children's books, available in Tibetan and European languages.

He founded the organisations:
Bodhicharya - see www.bodhicharya.org
and Rigul Trust - see www.rigultrust.org

Other books by Bodhicharya Publications

The Lazy Lama Series:

No. 1 - Buddhist Meditation

No. 2 - The Four Noble Truths

No. 3 - Refuge: Finding a Purpose and a Path

No. 4 - Bodhichitta: Awakening Compassion and Wisdom

No. 5 - Living without Fear and Anger

Heart Wisdom Series:

The Ngöndro: *Foundation Practices of Mahamudra*

From Milk to Yoghurt: *A Recipe for Living and Dying*

Like Dreams and Clouds: *Emptiness and Interdependence; Mahamudra and Dzogchen*

Dealing with Emotions: *Scattering the Clouds*

Journey from Head to Heart: *Along a Buddhist Path*

See: www.bodhicharya.org/publications

Rigul TrusT

Patron: Ringu Tulku Rinpoche

Rigul Trust is a UK charity whose objectives are the relief of poverty and financial hardship, the advancement of education, the advancement of religion, the relief of sickness, the preservation of good health.

Our main project is helping with health and education in Rigul, Tibet, the homeland of Ringu Tulku Rinpoche where his monastery is. We currently fund Dr Chuga, the nurse, the doctor's assistant, the running costs of the health clinic, the teachers, the cooks and the children's education plus two, free, hot meals a day at school.

We also help raise funds for disasters like earthquakes, floods, and help with schools in India and other health and welfare projects. All administration costs are met privately by volunteers.

100% OF ALL DONATIONS GOES TO FUND HEALTH, EDUCATION AND POVERTY RELIEF PROJECTS

Rigul Trust

13 St. Francis Avenue, Southampton, SO18 5QL U.K.

info@rigultrust.org

UK Charity Registration No: 1124076

TO FIND OUT MORE, OR MAKE A DONATION, PLEASE VISIT:

www.rigultrust.org

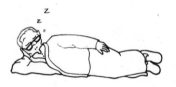

For an up to date list of books by Ringu Tulku,
please see the Books section at

www.bodhicharya.org